Contents

D0609863

A note on gender
The *'he'* pronoun is used throughout this book instead of the rather impersonal *'it'*, however no gender bias is intended.

Introduction

1. Taking on a puppy: Pros and cons

When you bring a puppy into your home, you can guarantee that life will never be the same again! A puppy is a bundle of fun, energy and mischief, and even though rearing a pup is a highly rewarding experience, it also demands a lot of hard work.

Before you make the final decision, weigh up all the pros and cons so you are confident that you can provide a suitable home. Remember, you are responsible for a dog's needs for the duration of his life, that means a commitment that will last for at least 10 years. A dog needs to be fed the correct diet; he needs grooming and exercise as well as preventative health care to ensure he remains fit and well.

In addition, you need to take on the role of leader, teaching your puppy his place in the family pack, training him in basic obedience and socialising him so that he becomes a model canine citizen.

'I can sense odours at concentrations nearly 1 million times lower than humans can.'

What will you get in return? The simple answer is that you will get back as much as you are prepared to put in. If you care for your dog correctly, spending time training and interacting with him, you will be rewarded with an outstanding companion. You will have a dog that is an integral member of your family, giving his own very special love and devotion. However, if you cut corners, skimping on daily care and never finding time for training, you will soon find you have a badly behaved dog that gives you little or no pleasure to own.

Make the right choice, and give your dog the time and attention he deserves. Start by reading this book, which will give you an introduction into what you need to know to be a responsible dog owner. Once you have mastered the basics, you will be well on the way to becoming your dog's best friend!

2. Origins & habitat

Latin name: Canis familiaris

It may be hard to believe, but all dogs – from the tiny Chihuahua to the giant Irish Wolfhound – are descended from the wolf.

No one knows exactly when wolves first became domesticated and joined the family circle, but fossil evidence from China indicates that this is a relationship that dates back some 15,000 years.

It is thought that the first dogs were descended from the Grey Wolf *(Canis lupis)*. These wolves lived in packs, hunting together and raising their cubs within the pack. No one can say why wolves joined forces with people. Maybe they were attracted by the warmth given out by the dying embers of a fire, or they may have discovered discarded scraps of food. But in time, wolves learnt to co-operate with man, helping in the hunt and guarding the home, in return for being given food and shelter.

These wolves would have bred together, producing offspring that had no fear of people, and who saw their natural place at man's side. Starting from a very few domesticated wolves, numbers quickly grew, as they proved how useful they could be. There were the hunters, tracking game by scent and by sight, there were those who herded and protected livestock, and those that guarded the family home.

By a process of selective breeding, the best characteristics were carried forward to future generations, and this was the start of creating dog breeds, with each breed being developed for a specific purpose.

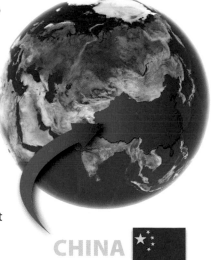

CHINA

There are now in excess of 400 million dogs around the world and Kennel Clubs worldwide recognise more than 800 different breeds.

Top tips

* Work out the cost in terms of time, money & commitment before taking on a puppy:

* You should not leave your dog on his own for more than 4 hrs a day.

* Give daily exercise. This is essential for all breeds, but if you get a livelier breed, your dog will need more.

* Time must be allocated for training & mental stimulation.

* All dogs require grooming; more so if you choose a longcoated breed.

* You need to afford veterinary bills which includes vaccinations, worming, flea treatments.

* Your dog needs a quality, well-balanced diet.

* If you go out to work, you may need to consider dog sitting expenses.

* If you go on holiday you may need the services of a boarding kennel.

3. Life span

Life expectancy can vary breed to breed.

10 years of age is an average of how long you can expect your dog to live for. Research into your specific breed for a more accurate estimate.

Perfect pet

4. Jobs for dogs

Dogs have been bred to carry out a vast range of jobs to help us in our daily lives. They include:

→→ Hunting dogs

In the past dogs, were bred to hunt many different animals, including deer, badger, otter and wild boar.

→→ Retrieving dogs

These dogs were developed to work with shooting parties, retrieving game over land and from water.

→→ Vermin catchers

The fearless terrier breeds prove their worth keeping down populations of mice and rats.

→→ Sheepdogs

Dogs that have a special ability to herd sheep, taking them to new pastures, and separating the flock when required.

→→ Livestock protectors

These dogs were used to look after the flock when they were grazing, protecting them from predators.

→→ Guard dogs

Big, powerful dogs that serve to guard the home and the family.

→→ Search and rescue dogs

Starting with the famous St Bernard, rescue dogs use their tracking skills to find people lost in natural disasters, such as earthquakes or avalanches.

→→ Sniffer dogs

Dogs that use their amazing sense of smell to detect drugs, arms and explosives.

→→ Assistance dogs

Dogs that are specially selected and trained to work with people with disabilities.

Dog world records

Oldest dog world record:
29 yrs 5 m A Queensland Heeler 'Bluey' USA.

Tallest dog world record:
107 cm (42.2 in) Great Dane 'Gibson' USA.

High jump world record:
172.7 cm (68 in) Greyhound Oct 7, '06.

Fastest dog record:
45 mph (72 km/h) Greyhound.

Did you know?

The dog's heart can beat up to 120 times per minute. That's 50% faster than the average heartbeat of a human.

Leader

5. The role of the leader

Although it is many thousands of years since wolves joined the family circle, we are lucky that dogs have retained many of the characteristics of a pack animal.

A wolf pack hunts together, each of the wolves working and co-operating with each other, and accepting the decisions of the pack leader. This is the best way of ensuring survival in the wild.

In the same way, a dog sees his family as his pack, and thrives on the companionship that is offered. However, a puppy needs to learn his place in the family so that he is happy to co-operate with all the pack members. This is particularly important in a family with young children.

First and foremost, a dog needs a leader he can respect, and who will teach him what is allowed, and what is not allowed in the home. This should not be viewed in a negative light, with the *'leader'* dishing out punishment and correction. It is a role of positive leadership, in which a dog is shown what is appropriate behaviour and is rewarded for co-operating. In this way, a dog accepts his place in the family, and has no desire to take over as leader.

Top tips

If you want to be a leader your dog will love and respect, try following these guidelines:

Start as you mean to go on: Don't wait until your puppy has become a boisterous *'teenager'* before training. You can start straight away.

Be consistent: Don't allow your puppy to jump on the sofa one moment because you want to give him a cuddle, and then tell him off next time he does it because he has muddy paws. A puppy only learns if he receives the same message on every occasion.

Be clear: Use the same cues/verbal commands so that he understands what you want.

Use your voice: When your puppy co-operates, praise him in a warm encouraging voice. When you want to stop undesirable behaviour, growl at him in a deep, stern voice. In this way, your puppy will learn *'right'* from *'wrong'.*

Curb unruly behaviour: If your puppy jumps up, or tries to nip, you must put a stop to it straightaway. Give a loud yelp, such as a puppy would do, to stop him mouthing, and then praise the pup if he allows you to stroke him quietly and calmly. If he tries to jump up, ignore him and only praise him when all four feet are on the ground.

Choosing the breed

6. The right choice

How do you decide which is the right breed for you and your family?

Breeds are divided into different groups depending on the role they were originally bred for, and this can also give you a clue as to the temperament they are most likely to inherit. Do as much homework as you can to find out about size, coat type, exercise requirements, potential health issues, as well as temperament and trainability before making your final choice.

7. Gundogs

Includes all the breeds that were bred to work as shooting companions.

They are divided into Retrievers *(e.g. Golden Retriever, Labrador Retriever),* Spaniels *(e.g. Cocker Spaniel, English Springer Spaniel),* Setters *(e.g. Irish Setter, English Setter),* Pointers, and Hunt, Point Retrieve *(HPR)* breeds *(e.g Weimaraner, German Shorthaired Pointer).*

They are active, intelligent dogs who respond well to all types of training. Gundogs generally make great family dogs and enjoy being included in all activities. Regular, varied exercise is essential.

8. Hounds

Includes Scenthounds *(e.g. Dachshunds, Bloodhounds, Beagles)* and Sighthounds *(e.g. Whippet, Greyhound, Saluki).*

Scenthounds were bred for their amazing sense of smell, and following a scent is their chief delight. Sighthounds are the true athletes of the canine world. They were bred to hunt by sight and can run at great speed.

Hounds are loyal companions, but they do not believe in instant obedience, so some patience is required. All hounds thrive on plenty of exercise.

9. Pastoral

Includes all breeds that were bred to work with livestock *(e.g. Border Collie, German Shepherd Dog, Old English Sheepdog).*

The majority of these breeds require an active lifestyle with lots of mental stimulation. Breeds such as the Border Collie and the German Shepherd Dog are the perfect choice if you want to take training to an advanced level.

Fun Fact!

The Greyhound is the fastest breed, reaching speeds of up to 45 mph (70 km/h), but at home he is a real couch potato.

10. Terriers

Includes hunting dogs that were bred go to ground in search of quarry *(e.g. Border Terrier, West Highland White Terrier)* and dogs that were originally bred for fighting *(e.g. Bull Terrier, Staffordshire Bull Terrier).*

Terriers are tough, feisty dogs that show great tenacity and courage. The former fighting dogs have fortunately left their history far behind and love being part of a family – although care needs to be taken when meeting other dogs. Terriers are quick-thinking and intelligent, so you need to keep one step ahead.

11. Toy

Includes the breeds that were bred specifically to be small, loving companions *(e.g. Bichon Frise, Cavalier King Charles Spaniel, Chihuahua).*

Despite their small size, Toy breeds should still be treated as proper dogs. They need mental stimulation and enjoy being included in all activities. These breeds thrive on human companionship and should not be taken on unless you can spend plenty of time with them.

12. Working

Includes guarding heavyweights *(e.g. Mastiff, Bullmastiff)*, Sled dogs *(e.g. Siberian Husky, Alaskan Malamute)*, and search and rescue dogs *(e.g. St Bernard).*

Breeds with strong guarding instincts need experienced handling, but they make loyal, impressive companions. Breeds that were used for sledding have tremendous powers of endurance and require a high activity lifestyle.

13. Utility

Includes a wide range of dogs bred for many different purposes. *(e.g. Shih Tzu, Dalmatian, Bulldog).*

The breeds in this group are so varied, you need to research your chosen breed to find out about temperament, trainability and individual care requirements.

14. Crossbreeds

If you take on a rescued dog you may well choose a crossbreed.

This is a dog with parents of two different breeds, such as a Labrador Retriever crossed with a Border Collie. Some breeders deliberately cross two breeds to create a new breed, such as the *Labradoodle,* which is a Labrador Retriever crossed with a Poodle.

Two puppies?

If you want more than one dog, you may be tempted to come home with two puppies from the same litter. But it is much better to wait until your first pup grows up and is fully trained before you take on a second.

Housing your puppy

15. A suitable home

There may be a shortlist of breeds that you think you might want to own. Before making your final choice, check out the following:

Size

Do you have a big enough home/garden for your chosen breed?

Coat care

Dogs have a range of different coat types ranging from low maintenance short coats *(e.g. Labrador Retriever),* to high maintenance long coated breeds *(e.g. Shih Tzu)* which require a huge amount of grooming. There are also breeds, such as the Poodle, which need regular trips to the grooming parlour to have their coats clipped.

Money

You need to cover all the costs involved in owning a dog *(food, veterinary care, boarding etc.).* A large dog will eat more food and will therefore will be more expensive to keep.

Time

No dog should be left for more than four hours a day, but some breeds are more needy than others. Work out how much time you can spend with a dog before making your choice.

Trainability

If you have ambitions to take part in one of the canine sports, such as *Competitive Obedience* or *Agility*, choose a breed that will enjoy the challenge of advanced training.

Finding a puppy

Top tips

Kennel Club

To find out more about different dog breeds and where to locate breeders, log on to the Kennel Club website:

www.the-kennel-club. org.uk or www.akc.org

✔

16. Locating a breeder

Once you have decided on a breed to suit your lifestyle, you need to find a breeder who has a reputation for producing healthy puppies that are typical of the breed.

Start by contacting specialist breed clubs to find out where breeders are located and who has puppies available.

17. Assessing the puppies

When you visit a litter of puppies, check that their environment is clean and hygienic, and that the puppies are lively and appear healthy.

You will also want to see the mother with her puppies so you can get an idea of the temperament they are likely to inherit.

18. Leaving home

In most cases, the breeder will let you take your puppy home when he is around eight weeks of age.

In the case of 'Toy' breeds, the breeder may prefer to wait until the pups are a little older and stronger before going to their new homes.

19. Health issues

There are a number of genetic conditions that can be inherited by dogs.

These are often breed specific, so it is important to find out about any inherited conditions which exist within your chosen breed. Breeding stock must have clearances for inherited conditions, so make sure you check the paperwork with the breeder.

20. A healthy puppy

Look for the following signs of good health and sound temperament:

→ Eyes

These should be wide, bright and alert. There shouldn't be any signs of fluid discharge from the eye. They should be clear, shining and full of life.

→ Ears

The ears are clean with no trace of bad odour. Check that the pups respond to different types of sound.

→ Teeth

The teeth should be clean, and the gums free from sores, bleeding or inflammation.

→ Nose

The nose has no sign of crustiness or discharge.

→ Coat

The puppies' coats look clean and they smell fresh (i.e. They do not smell of urine or faeces).

→ Body

All the pups are nicely covered without appearing too fat or too thin. A pot-bellied pup may be carrying a burden of worms. (p23 'Internal parasites'). The puppies should move effortlessly, with no signs of limping or lameness.

→ Claws

These should be level with the pad, curved rather than straight and should not be too long. The puppy should not have any broken claws nor any damage to the dew claws (front and rear, if they have not been removed already).

→ Temperament

The puppies are alert and playful, and are happy to come up and greet you.

→ Rear

The rear end is clean (matted fur could indicate diarrhoea).

Choosing your puppy

21. The stud dog

You are unlikely to meet the father *(sire)* of the puppies, as breeders often travel a considerable distance to use a stud dog that will complement their bitch. But you should ask to see a photo, as well as enquiring about his temperament.

22. Male or female?

Whether you choose a male or a female *(bitch)* is very much a matter of personal preference. In the majority of breeds, the male is bigger than the female, which may be a consideration.

If you choose a bitch you will have to cope with her seasonal cycle. A bitch comes in season every six to nine months, and during this three-week period she must be kept away from male dogs unless you plan to breed with her.

In terms of temperament, it is almost impossible to generalise as all dogs are individuals. In large breeds with a guarding instinct *(e.g; Rottweiler, German Shepherd Dog, Boxer),* the male can be more dominant and first-time owners would do better to opt for a bitch.

Getting ready

23. Home check

While you are waiting to collect your puppy, you can spend time preparing for the new arrival.

You need to make sure that your house is 100 per cent safe as an inquisitive puppy can get himself into trouble. Look at your home from a puppy's perspective and remove potential hazards such as trailing wires, house plants or breakable ornaments. Make sure all items of value are stored out of your puppy's reach.

24. Security alert

Check the garden and make sure it is safe and secure.

There should be no gaps in the fencing and if you have a gate, it should have a secure fastening. If you have a garden pond, it will need to be fenced off or covered
until your puppy is older.

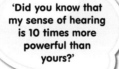

'Did you know that my sense of hearing is 10 times more powerful than yours?'

Top tips

Plants

There are a number of plants that are poisonous to dogs.

The best plan is to seek advice from your local garden centre, or to do some research on the internet.

Plants that are toxic to dogs include the following:

- Azalea
- Daffodil
- Elderberry
- Foxglove
- Holly
- Hyacinth
- Iris
- Laurel
- Lily Of The Valley
- Milkweed
- Mistletoe
- Nightshade
- Oleander
- Primrose
- Ragwort
- Rhododendron
- Stinging Nettle
- Wisteria
- Yew

Housing your puppy

25. Sleeping quarters

First of all, you will need to decide where your puppy is going to sleep. Most owners use the kitchen or utility room.

Make sure the place you choose is free from draughts and does not get too hot or too cold. A conservatory is not suitable as the temperature can rise in the day and then fall dramatically at night.

26. Indoor crate

The best type of accommodation for a puppy is an indoor crate.

This provides a safe base for your pup, which he will regard as his own special den. It can be used to keep your puppy contained overnight and at other times when he cannot be supervised. Make sure the crate you buy is big enough to accommodate an adult dog. Line the crate with synthetic fleece bedding to make it cosy. This type of bedding is machine washable and is easy to dry.

27. Dog bed

If you want to provide an additional bed for your puppy, for example, in the sitting room, choose a plastic kidney shaped bed, which is chew resistant, and line it with bedding.

28. Collar and lead

Your puppy should get used to wearing a collar from an early stage.

Buy a soft, lightweight collar so he will hardly notice he is wearing it. Your pup will grow fast, so it makes sense to buy an adjustable collar which you can use until he reaches his full size. Buy a lightweight lead to begin with; making sure it has a secure trigger fastening.

29. Grooming gear

The equipment you need will depend on your dog's coat, so ask the breeder for advice.

In the first few weeks, all you need is a soft brush so your puppy can get used to being groomed.

30. Toys

You will have great fun choosing toys for your puppy – and he will certainly enjoy playing with them.

However, you must make sure that the toys you buy are completely safe. The best type are cotton raggers and kongs, which are made of hard rubber. If you choose squeaky toys or soft toys, your puppy should be supervised when he is playing.

1. Indoor crate.
2. Kidney shaped dog bed.
3. Grooming brush.
4. Comb.
5. Toothpaste/ Brush.
6. Dog Identity tag.

Identification

In the U.K, it is a legal requirement for dogs to wear some form of ID.

You can get a disc engraved with your name, address and postcode, and attach it to the collar. You may also want to consider a permanent form of ID, such as microchipping. This simple procedure is usually carried out by a veterinary.

The puppy food guide

31. Starting right

When you collect your puppy, the breeder will probably give you enough food to last for the first few days.

It is important to stick to this diet to avoid the risk of an upset stomach. You may decide to keep to this diet, or you may prefer to look at what else is on offer. Remember that if you change diets, you must do so gradually, adding a little more of the new food at every meal until you have made a complete switch.

32. What's on offer?

➔➔ Complete

This is an easy diet to feed and caters for all nutritional requirements as a puppy is growing. You can then swap on to an adult diet, which will be lower in protein.

➔➔ Canned

Canned meat is usually fed with biscuit. Dogs find it very appetising, but the content can vary considerably in nutritional value, so you will need to check the label.

➔➔ Fresh Food:

Some owners prefer to feed a homemade diet, or to follow the BARF diet *(Biologically Appropriate Raw Food or Bones)*. This can work well, but requires a lot of input from the owner to keep a supply of fresh food and to ensure the diet has the correct nutritional balance.

Whatever diet, you choose, remember that fresh water should be available at all times.

33. Chews

Most dogs enjoy gnawing on a bone or a chew.

This is beneficial as it exercises the jaws and helps to keep the teeth clean. Puppies who are teething often find that chewing eases the discomfort they are feeling. However, bones can splinter and cause serious problems so avoid giving cooked bones. The best plan is to seek advice from the staff in your local pet store to find out what bones and chews are most suitable for your type of dog.

1.

2.

34. Mealtimes

In most cases, a puppy will need four meals a day to start with. This will decrease as he grows older.

Most adult dogs are fed twice daily. Do not worry if your pup is reluctant to eat when he first arrives in his new home. It is simply that he has so much to get used to; he cannot concentrate on his food. He may also miss the competition of feeding with his littermates.

Leave the food down for 10 minutes, and then remove the bowl and start with fresh food at the next meal. Most puppies soon get their appetites back. However, if you have any concerns, seek advice from your veterinary.

3.

4.

35. Bowls

You will need two bowls – one for food and one for water.

The best type to buy are those made of stainless steel as they are easy to clean and they are virtually indestructible.

Top tips

Dangers of obesity

It is all too easy for a dog to put on excess weight if he is fed too much at mealtimes, or if he is given too many treats.

The aim is to feed the correct amount of food to suit your dog's age, size and lifestyle. If you are using treats for training, deduct them from your dog's daily ration so you can monitor how much food he is getting. You can also use healthy treats, such as pieces of carrot, which most dogs love.

Remember, an obese dog can suffer from severe health problems which will shorten life expectancy, so it is your job to keep a close check on your dog's weight. If you have any concerns, ask your veterinary for advice.

5.

6.

7.

1. Canned dog food.
2. Edible dog ball.
3. Dog food bowl.
4. Dog water bowl.
5. Training treats.
6. Dog chew bone.
7. Nutritionally complete, dried dog food.

Arriving home

36. Meeting the family

At last the big day arrives when it is time to collect your puppy.

This is exciting for the family, but it can be very daunting for a puppy to arrive in a new home which is full of strangers. Try not to overwhelm your puppy; give him a chance to explore his surroundings and find his feet in his new home.

If you have young children, you will need to supervise all interactions. Children should sit on the floor when they are stroking or cuddling a puppy as this prevents the risk of a wriggly pup being dropped. Give each child a treat and let the pup take it gently. You can also introduce some toys, but make sure play does not become too boisterous.

37. Introducing other pets

If you already have a dog, allow the pup and the resident dog to meet in the garden.

To start with, keep the older dog on the lead so there is no danger of the pup being bowled over. Then let him off lead, and allow the two dogs to meet each other. Check the resident dog if he is too rough, but try to allow the pair to get to know each other without too much interference.

A dog and a cat can learn to live in harmony, but take great care with initial introductions. Start by letting the pup meet the cat when she is safely confined in a carrier. This gives the pup a chance to go up and investigate, but as the cat is not moving he will not be tempted to give chase. Every now and then, call the pup, and reward him for coming away from the cat.

The next step is to introduce the pair when the cat is out of the carrier. The cat will feel safer if he is on a higher surface, such as a chair or a table, so he is out of reach. Keep a close check on your pup so that he does not attempt to jump up at the cat, and, again, reward, him when he responds to you rather than becoming focused on the cat. You will have to repeat this scenario on a number of occasions but, in time, your puppy will learn that cats are not for chasing.

If you have small pets, such as rabbits, you must ensure that their accommodation is 100 per cent secure, and make sure the pup is never left unsupervised in their presence.

Top tips

Puppies & children

Puppies and children are a great mix as long as you observe some important guidelines:

Do not allow your pup to mouth or nip or jump up, as he will think he can play rough in the same way as he did with his littermates.

Teach children to stroke the puppy gently so they learn not to pinch, tug or torment him in any other way.

Supervise play sessions and make sure children do not become over-excited as this will encourage your pup to become unruly.

Keep children's toys out of reach so your pup learns that he can only play with his own toys.

When your puppy is sleeping or eating, he should not be disturbed.

Early lessons

38. Handling

Your puppy should get used to being handled from an early age so that he accepts being groomed and being examined by a veterinary.

Start by stroking him all over, moving your hands over his head, down his back, along his underside, and then moving to his hindquarters and tail. Then pick up each paw in turn and check the toes, nails and pads. Stroke the ears, and look inside, checking they are clean and free from odour. Finally, part the lips and check the teeth and gums. Some puppies wriggle a bit to begin with, but if you are firm, but gentle, most will soon co-operate. Remember to reward your puppy with a treat at the end of each handling session.

39. Sit

This is an easy exercise to teach!

You can start as soon as your puppy arrives in your home. Hold a treat just above his nose, and as he looks up, he will naturally lower his hindquarters and go into a *Sit*. Reward your pup and repeat a couple more times. When your pup is responding every time, you can introduce the verbal cue *"Sit"*. In time, your pup will respond to the cue and you will not need to use a lure.

40. Down

When you pup has learnt to *Sit*, you can progress to the *Down* position.

Start with your puppy sitting, and show him that you have a treat. Close your hand over the treat and slowly lower it towards the floor. The pup will follow the treat, and will lower his forequarters and then his hindquarters as he tries to reach it. As soon as he is in the *Down* position, reward him with the treat. You will need to practise this a few times before your pup gets the idea. Do not introduce the verbal cue *"Down"* until your pup is responding every time you lure him into position.

41. Come

A puppy will naturally want to follow you, so start off from day one, calling the pup to *"Come"* and then giving him a treat.

You can play a game, with a helper holding on to the pup, and releasing him the moment you call. Work at the exercise at home where there are fewer distractions and build up a strong response before attempting it in a more challenging environment.

42. Walking on a lead

This takes quite a bit of practice but it is well worth the effort when you are rewarded with a dog that is happy to walk with you on a loose lead. You can start work at home while you are waiting for your pup to complete his vaccination programme.

→ First accustom your puppy to wearing a collar. Try putting it on just before a mealtime so his attention will be focused on his food rather than scratching at his collar.

→ Next attach a lead, and allow your pup to wonder at will, making sure the lead does not become entangled.

→ Try picking up the end of the lead and following your pup so that he get used to being *'attached'* to you.

→ The next step is to encourage your pup to walk with you rather than taking his own line. Use a treat so your pup wants to follow you, and after a few paces reward him. Build this up gradually until your pup understands that he is being rewarded for walking alongside you. You can then introduce the verbal cue *"Heel"* or *"Close"*.

* Now try some circles and changes of direction, remembering to give lots of encouragement and rewarding on a regular basis. Keep practising, and you will be off to a good start when your puppy is ready to venture into the outside world.

43. Stay

This exercise should be built up in easy stages so your pup learns to stay in position until you release him.

Start with your puppy on the lead and place him in a *Down* – he is more likely to stay in this position rather than a *Sit*. Stand in front of him and take one step away. Use a hand signal by holding your hand up, palm facing the puppy, effectively *'blocking'* his progress. Return to your puppy and reward him. Next time, try two steps back, and then maybe a couple of steps to the side so the puppy learns that he must stay in position regardless of where you are standing. When your pup has got the idea of staying in position, introduce the verbal cue *"Stay"*. With practice, your puppy will learn to *"Stay"* off lead for an extended period.

44. Socialisation

As well as training your puppy in basic obedience, you need to give him an all round education so he becomes a well-balanced, canine citizen.

This process is known as socialisation and it involves taking your puppy to different environments and giving him the chance to experience as many different sights and sounds as possible. A puppy soaks up new experiences like a sponge and if he is given a comprehensive programme of socialisation, with encouragement and support when needed, he will mature into an adult dog that will react calmly and confidently in all situations.

Exercise

Top tips

Swimming

Swimming is a great form of exercise which many dogs enjoy. Make sure you find a safe stretch of water which is not too deep and without strong currents. You also need to make sure there is easy access in and out of the water.

45. How much exercise?

In the first few months, your puppy will get as much exercise as he needs playing in the garden.

In fact, it is very important not to over- exercise puppies – particularly medium to large size breeds – as their bones and joints are vulnerable while they are growing. When a dog has finished growing he will still enjoy a variety of exercise which includes lead exercise and free running. If you have a Toy breed, your dog may not need a lot of exercise, but he will appreciate the opportunity to explore new places.

46. Games to play

A puppy will enjoy playing with toys, and also playing games with members of the family.

This provides mental stimulation, physical exercise, plus the opportunity to spend time interacting with his human *'pack'*. Try teaching your pup to retrieve a toy, to play hide and seek in the garden *(you hide, and then call your pup to you)*, or lay a treasure trail by hiding treats that he has to find. You can also teach him some fun tricks such as offering his paw for a handshake, or weaving through your legs.

Health care

47. Vaccinations

Your puppy will need to be vaccinated against a number of infectious diseases.

These include:
Canine adenovirus | Distemper | Leptospirosis | Parvovirus

Vaccinations are also available for **Rabies** which your dog will need if you plan to travel overseas with him, and **Kennel Cough** which you will need if your dog is going to boarding kennels.

In most cases, the vaccination course starts at eight weeks and is completed at 10 weeks. However, this varies, depending on your veterinary and the incidence of disease in your area.

48. Best friends

As we have seen, taking on a puppy is a major undertaking, but if you keep your half of the bargain and spend time training, socialising and caring for your pup, you will be rewarded with a loyal and loving companion that you are proud to own.

Regular care

→ Internal parasites

There are a number of internal parasites that affect dogs.

The most common in the U.K are roundworm and tapeworm. The breeder will have started a worming programme and you will need to continue with this throughout your dog's life. Ask your veterinary for specialist advice.

→ External parasites

Fleas are the most common of the external parasites that affect dogs, but ticks can also be a problem depending on where you live.

There is effective spot on treatment which should be administered on a routine basis to keep the problem of external parasites at bay.

→ Routine care

Your dog should be groomed on a regular basis, even if he has a low maintenance coat, as this gives you the opportunity to check him for lumps or bumps, or any sign of soreness or discomfort.

If you spot a problem at an early stage, the veterinary has a far greater chance of treating it successfully.

→ Teeth

These will need to be cleaned routinely to cope with the build up of tartar and prevent gum disease.

→ Ears

Examine the inside of the ears and clean if necessary, making sure you do not probe into the ear canal.

If you pup is shaking his head or scratching his ears, he may have ear mites or an ear infection which will need to be treated by a veterinary.

→ Eyes

These should be bright and sparkling, and free from discharge. If the eye appears red or inflamed, or has a discharge, seek veterinary advice.

→ Nails

Nails should not be allowed to grow too long, as this can be very uncomfortable and can cause lameness.

You can trim the nails using guillotine type nail clippers, but if you are worried about doing this, you can ask a veterinary or a veterinary nurse to do the job for you.

Other titles

magnet® **&**
steel
publishing limited

Magnet & Steel Publishing Ltd
Unit 6
Vale Business Park,
Llandow, United Kingdom. CF71 7PF
sales@magnetandsteelpublishing.com